Health Care

How Can We Bring Costs Down While Getting the Care We Need?

HIGH HEALTH-CARE COSTS affect all Americans, often in deeply personal ways. This guide is designed to help people deliberate together about how we should approach the issue. It suggests three options for deliberation, along with the trade-offs each might involve. Each option presents advantages as well as downsides. Each raises questions for which there are no easy answers.

- If we create a single government program to pay for everyone's health care, would taxes rise and quality suffer?
- Can gradual reforms hold costs down and still get everybody covered?
- Should we take responsibility for our own choices in a more transparent and competitive marketplace even if that means those who make poor decisions will suffer the consequences?

Improving the US health-care system routinely presents choices between holding the line on enormous costs, covering more people, and maintaining the choices and quality of care Americans deserve. Which should be our priority?

Introduction

AMERICANS, INDIVIDUALLY AND AS A NATION, are worried about high health-care costs. Whether we have insurance or not, many of us fear that skyrocketing drug prices and surprise medical bills could keep us from getting the care we need or ruin us financially. Businesses and governments also face increasing costs.

We pay more for health care than other countries do but have less to show for it. Overall, the United States spent more than $11,000 per person on health care in 2018. That figure includes what individuals paid, what businesses paid, and what federal, state, and local governments paid.

Other wealthy countries spend about half as much as the United States does—on average, $5,280 per person. Yet people in France, Canada, Australia, and other countries with similar economies are healthier and live longer than Americans.

Health Insurance Coverage of the US Population

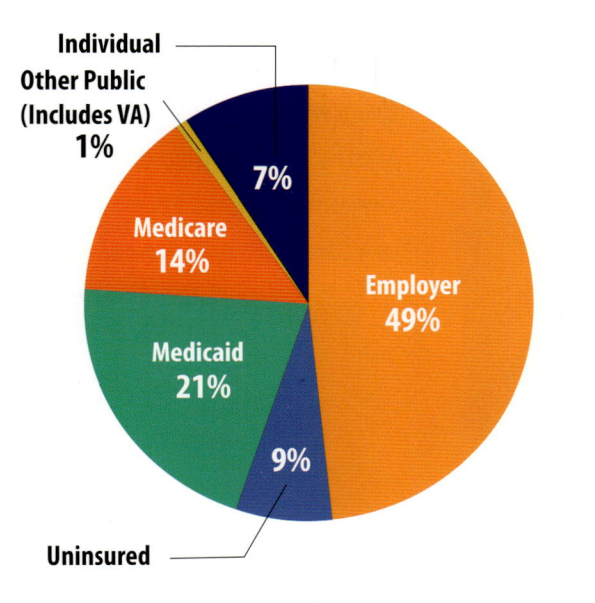

- Individual Other Public (Includes VA) 1%
- Employer 49%
- Uninsured 9%
- Medicaid 21%
- Medicare 14%
- 7%

Source: *Kaiser Family Foundation*, 2017

US Health Care: Higher Costs, Poorer Results Than Other High-Income Nations

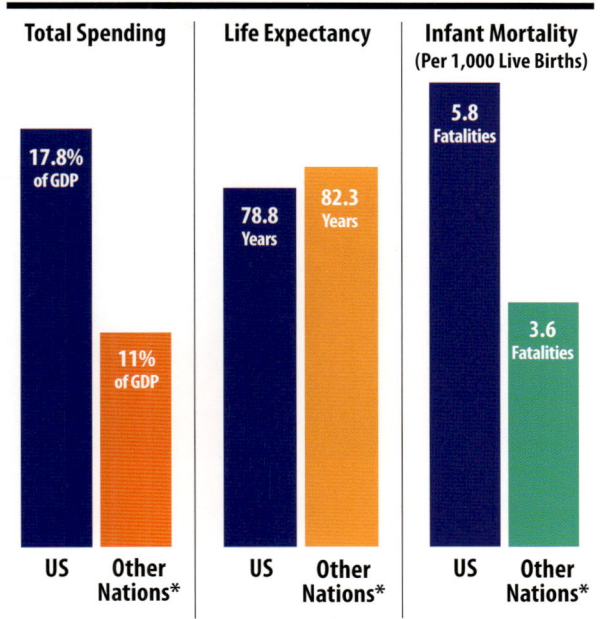

Total Spending		Life Expectancy		Infant Mortality (Per 1,000 Live Births)	
17.8% of GDP	11% of GDP	78.8 Years	82.3 Years	5.8 Fatalities	3.6 Fatalities
US	Other Nations*	US	Other Nations*	US	Other Nations*

* UK, Canada, Australia, Japan, Sweden, France, Denmark, Netherlands, Switzerland, Germany (average)

Source: *Journal of the American Medical Association*, 2016

The way we pay for health care is complicated. More than half of Americans are covered by private insurance, mostly job based. About one-third are covered by government programs. These include Medicare (for seniors), Medicaid (for people with very low income), and military care. Some 9 percent of the population—28 million people—had no insurance at all in 2017.

Prices are unpredictable and confusing. Insurance companies negotiate rates with hospitals, doctors, and other providers. Health-care costs vary widely between states as well as within cities. A common blood test in Beaumont, Texas, costs $443, nearly 25 times more than the same test in Toledo, Ohio, where it costs $18. In Dallas alone, hospital charges for a total knee replacement range from $16,772 to $61,587.

The US health insurance system has developed over decades. Employers began offering health insurance during World War II. In 1965, Congress enacted Medicare and Medicaid. The 2010 Affordable Care Act expanded Medicaid, created "marketplaces" for buying private insurance, required insurance companies to accept people with preexisting conditions, and made other reforms.

Health-care costs have been rising faster than inflation for years, and even though the Affordable Care Act broadened coverage, millions of Americans remain uninsured. No wonder a recent Gallup poll found that health care still

©John Moore/Getty Images

People wait to enter the Remote Area Medical (RAM) mobile clinic in 2017 in Wise, Virginia. This is one of many free weekend clinics RAM holds in Appalachia, providing dental, medical, and vision services to thousands of uninsured and underinsured people.

"tops the list of Americans' worries." One in four said they had skipped treatment because of the costs, and 77 percent said that rising costs will damage the US economy.

Meanwhile, government spending on health care also continues to rise. The federal government already spends a quarter of its budget on health care. This is more than it spends on defense.

This issue guide presents three options for reforming our health-care system, and each option presents advantages as well as risks. The guide does not include every idea currently under discussion, but the basic questions in this guide can help people think through other proposals.

The research involved in developing this guide included a review of policy ideas from across the political spectrum, interviews and conversations with Americans from all walks of life, and reviews of initial drafts by experts with experience in this area.

Option 1:
Ensure Health Care for All

ALEC SMITH WAS JUST 26 when he fell into a diabetic coma and died alone in his Minnesota apartment. His mother discovered too late that he had begun rationing the life-saving insulin he needed for his type 1 diabetes. Like 28 million Americans, Alec didn't have health insurance. And without insurance covering his drugs or offering discounted prices for them, he was charged the full list price: a staggering $1,300 a month.

"Being the proud 26-year-old, trying to be an independent young man, he didn't call mom and dad for help," Nicole Smith-Holt told the Minneapolis *Star Tribune*. "He thought, 'Maybe I could take a little less insulin. Maybe I could miss a dose. Maybe I could change my diet. Maybe I could stretch this out till payday.'"

This option says that all Americans deserve health-care coverage as a basic right, and the fairest way to provide it is to create a government health insurance program similar to Medicare that

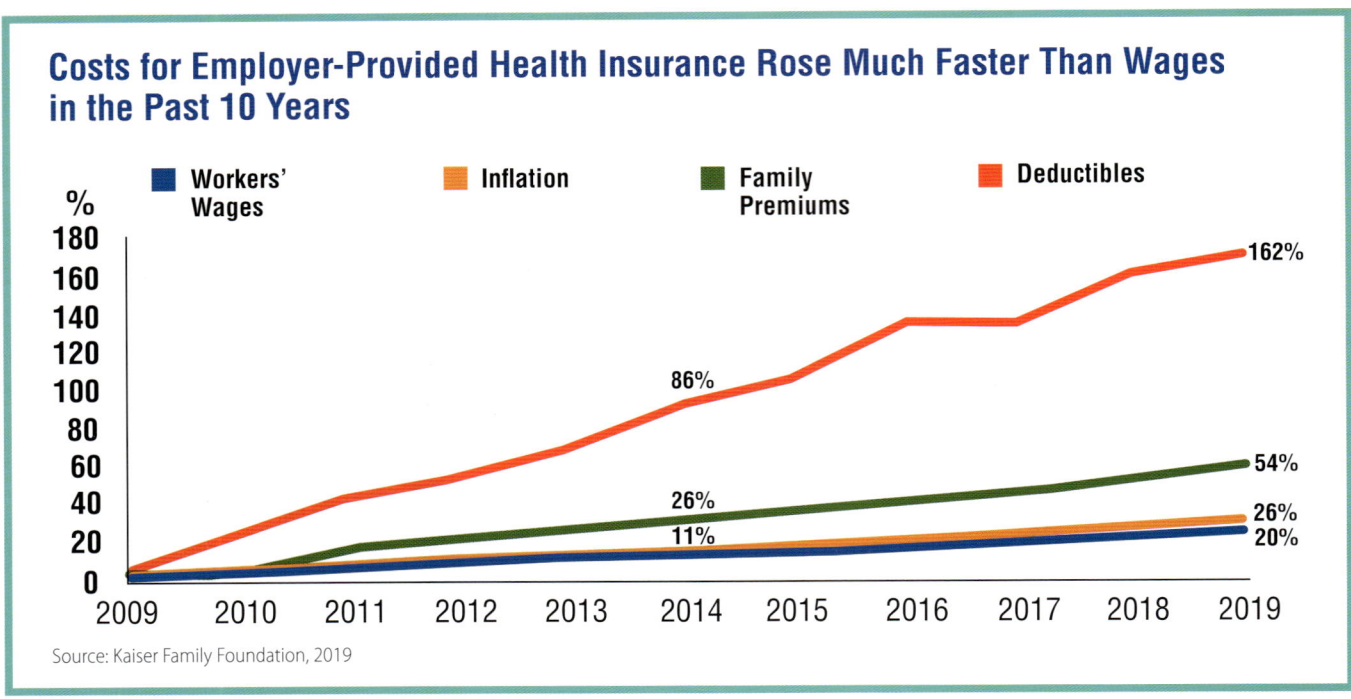

Costs for Employer-Provided Health Insurance Rose Much Faster Than Wages in the Past 10 Years

Source: Kaiser Family Foundation, 2019

covers everybody, regardless of job, income, or medical history.

The patchwork of private and public plans we have now leaves too many people like Alec falling through the cracks. At 26, he was too old for his mother's insurance, where his insulin had cost him $300 a month. His restaurant job didn't offer health benefits. And he earned too much to qualify for the low-income Medicaid program or for subsidies that would have made an individual policy affordable.

Even with insurance, many Americans are not fully protected against high costs, often paying ever-rising monthly premiums. Almost half of insured Americans have "high-deductible" coverage. That means they must pay thousands of dollars out of their own pockets before insurance even kicks in. On average, according to the nonpartisan Kaiser Family Foundation, employer-sponsored plans come with a $1,655 deductible. And an eighth (13 percent) of covered workers have a deductible higher than $3,000.

For many Americans, there is near-constant confusion over what services are covered and at what cost. People can be hit with surprise bills if they inadvertently go to doctors or hospitals outside their policy's network of health-care providers.

What we have now amounts to a two-tiered health-care system. Americans with comfortable incomes have access to the best the US system has to offer. A great many others, however, cannot afford the high-priced specialists, costly medical procedures, and expensive drugs available to their fellow Americans who make more money. They wait longer for care, ration their medications, or, for some, must rely on emergency room visits.

This option says that a single government insurance program would be more cost-effective, easier to navigate, and fairer to all.

A Primary Drawback of This Option:

This is a drastic overhaul of our system that would eliminate private, job-based insurance, which now covers 181 million Americans. It would create a huge new government bureaucracy responsible for our health care.

What We Should Do

Immediately bring the 28 million people who do not have health insurance into a new government plan similar to Medicare.

Uninsured adults are 40 percent more likely to die early than people with insurance even after taking into account such factors as education, income, smoking, drinking, and obesity, according to a study published in the *American Journal of Public Health*.

This option says that we could make our health-care system fairer by immediately enrolling all uninsured Americans in a new public plan similar to Medicare. Elderly Americans already have such a safety net, and very low-income adults and almost all poor children have Medicaid.

Move people with private and job-based insurance onto the government plan.

Right now, about $266 billion of the $3.5 trillion that the United States spends on health care goes into administration. Doctors and hospitals devote a tremendous amount of time and resources to billing, collecting payments, and negotiating with both government and private insurers, each with its own set of rules and forms.

"The extraordinary costs we see are not because of administrative slack or because health-care leaders don't try to economize," Dr. Kevin Schulman, a professor of medicine at North Carolina's Duke University, told the *New York Times*. "The high administrative costs are functions of the system's complexity."

It's time to simplify the system. This option says that we can do so by sweeping away private and employer-based insurance entirely and starting fresh with a single, Medicare-like insurance plan for all Americans.

New Englanders Glenn and Tracy McCarthy look over a pile of medical bills they could not pay after their health insurance changed. A recent Harvard University study shows that high medical bills are a leading cause of personal bankruptcy in the United States.

©Matthew J. Lee/The Boston Globe via Getty Images

Use government's purchasing power to make hospitals, doctors, and drug companies drop prices and keep them down.

According to this option, the reason Americans pay more is not because care is better here. Many other countries deliver better care at lower cost. But since the governments of these other countries bargain on behalf of every patient, they do better at making hospitals, doctors, and drug companies keep costs reasonable. They negotiate prices or set overall budgets for what they will pay for all health services, depending on population size and needs or on diagnosis or outcome. This option says the United States should do the same.

Outlaw astronomical jury awards for malpractice.

Doctors have long complained that fear of malpractice lawsuits forces them to protect themselves by ordering unnecessary tests and procedures. The costs of the tests as well as the high costs of malpractice insurance get passed on.

A recent study by economists from Duke University and the Massachusetts Institute of Technology confirmed that this kind of "defensive medicine" boosts hospital costs.

Researchers compared care between otherwise similar military and civilian hospitals. Military hospitals cannot be sued. They ordered fewer tests, yet offered the same quality of care as their civilian counterparts.

More than 25 states now have laws that limit medical liability cases. This option says that to discourage unnecessary defensive care, such reforms should be extended nationwide.

Provo, Utah, obstetrician and gynecologist Dr. Jefforey Thorpe holds an arbitration agreement in which patients may waive the right to sue the doctor and agree to submit any dispute to arbitration. Doctors around the nation use these agreements at the urging of their insurance companies to reduce the cost of malpractice insurance. In some instances, these forms are mandatory.

©George Frey/Getty Images

Trade-Offs and Downsides

■ The United States is already deeply in debt and can't afford a vast new government benefit to cover some 28 million people even if the new system is more effective at holding down costs. We will probably still need to pay higher taxes. And quality could be threatened if the government pushes hospitals and doctors to reduce their costs too much.

■ Eliminating private insurance would leave 181 million people no choice but to join a public plan whether they want to or not.

■ Using government power to force prices down interferes with the marketplace and hinders new drug development.

■ Medical errors kill up to 250,000 Americans a year. Capping malpractice awards would eliminate a tool for making sure doctors and hospitals are more careful.

Questions for deliberation . . .

1 This option gives government more responsibility for the health-care system. Do you think that government would do a better job than private insurers do now? Why or why not?

2 Moving from our current system, which includes government and private insurance, to a single government-managed insurance system such as Medicare for All would be a major change. For instance, many jobs in the insurance industry would be lost. What other kinds of unintended consequences should we worry about?

3 We already provide care for people who can't pay at the nation's public hospitals and clinics. Do we need to do more, and if so, why?

Option 2:
Build on What We Have

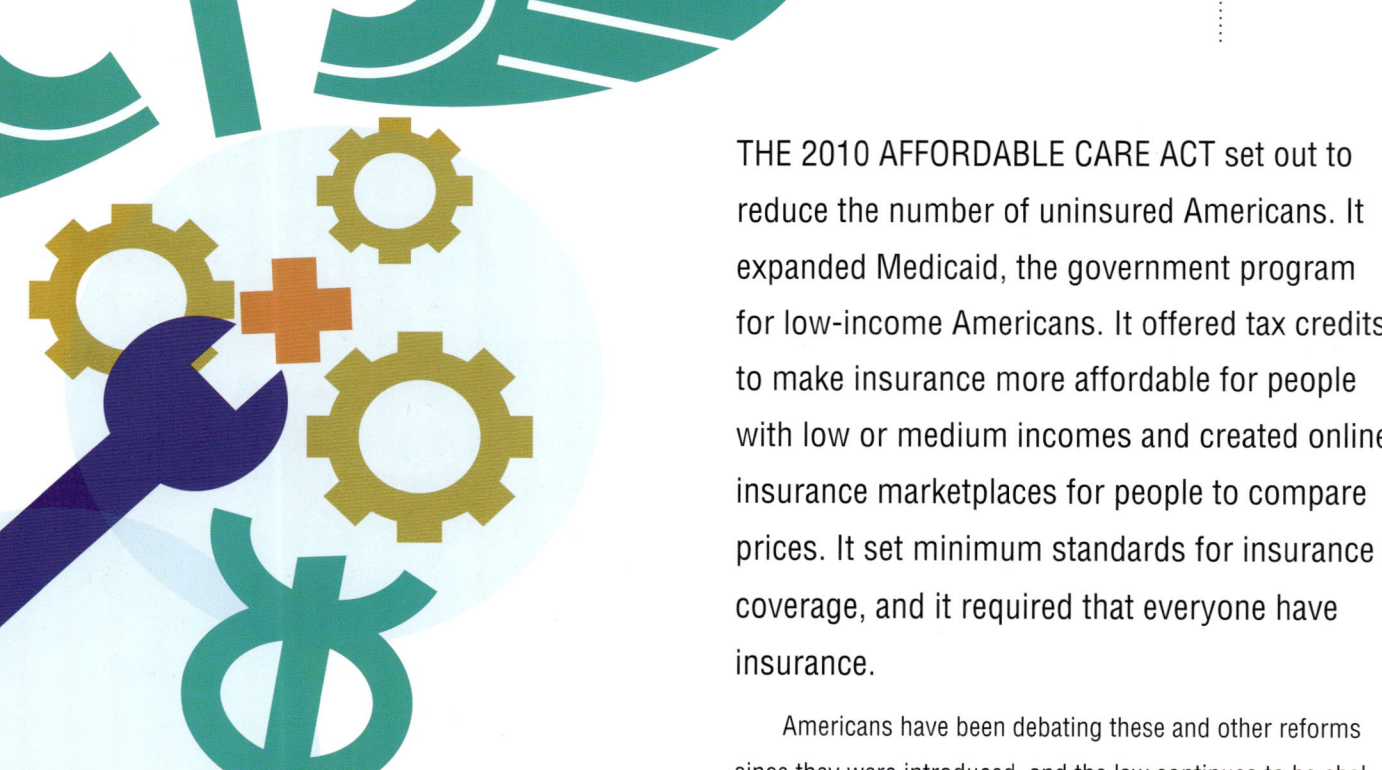

THE 2010 AFFORDABLE CARE ACT set out to reduce the number of uninsured Americans. It expanded Medicaid, the government program for low-income Americans. It offered tax credits to make insurance more affordable for people with low or medium incomes and created online insurance marketplaces for people to compare prices. It set minimum standards for insurance coverage, and it required that everyone have insurance.

Americans have been debating these and other reforms since they were introduced, and the law continues to be challenged in court. But parts of it have become widely popular. Young people can now stay on their parents' insurance up to age 26. And no one can be denied coverage due to a preexisting condition. Previously, people could be refused insurance or charged extra because of conditions such as diabetes, depression, or a history of cancer.

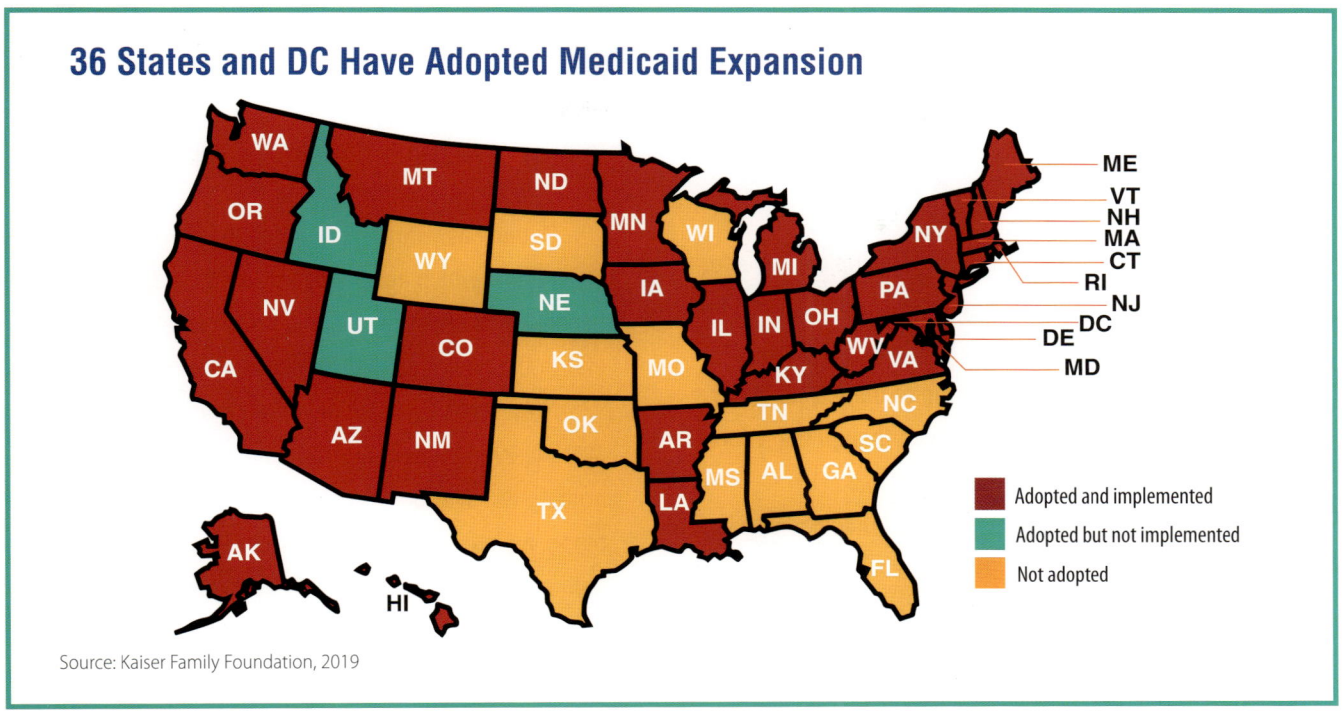

36 States and DC Have Adopted Medicaid Expansion

Legend:
- Adopted and implemented
- Adopted but not implemented
- Not adopted

Source: Kaiser Family Foundation, 2019

Since the law was fully implemented in 2014, the number of people with no coverage has dropped from 44 million to 28 million. More than 90 percent of Americans are now insured.

This option says that we should build on this progress rather than start over. We should fix what's broken, not dismantle the system currently in place.

Take the people who still fall through the cracks because they're unable to afford an individual policy but earn too much for public assistance. More people could get coverage if we required all states to accept Medicaid expansion. A number have not.

Yet even if the Affordable Care Act were working as planned, many Americans would face daunting costs. A study by the Commonwealth Fund research organization estimates that as many as 44 million Americans with insurance are having a hard time paying out-of-pocket costs. As spiraling drug prices and hospital charges get passed on to people through higher premiums, more people resort to high-deductible plans or find insurance unaffordable altogether. Employers, too, find it difficult to offer insurance or must offer only no-frills plans.

We also need to find better ways to keep overall costs down whether they're paid privately or by the government. We might start by encouraging healthier habits and working with patients and families to rein in the costliest care of all—that which occurs in the last few months of life.

This option says the best way to both cover more people and protect them from high prices is to strengthen the 2010 Affordable Care Act. Improving the mix of private and public options we already have, in this view, is the safest and least disruptive way to bring down costs and still get the good health care we deserve.

A Primary Drawback of This Option:

Keeping the private insurance system we have now does not directly address costs, nor does it help people navigate a confusing and wasteful system.

What We Should Do

Expand Medicaid in every state to cover working people without insurance as well as the very poor.

The Affordable Care Act made more people eligible for Medicaid by raising the income cutoff to about $26,000 for a family of four. A Supreme Court ruling left the decision about whether to expand Medicaid up to the states. Today, 14 states have refused to go along even though the federal government would have paid most of the bill.

Studies show that in states that expanded coverage, fewer infants died and more cancers were diagnosed earlier. More people were able to get care for mental health problems and opioid addiction. Emergency room use declined. And that meant that hospitals suffered fewer financial hits from unpaid bills.

Require everyone to have health insurance so it will be more affordable overall.

The 2010 reform law required that everybody have insurance. But effective in 2019, Congress eliminated the tax penalty for those who don't comply, arguing that young,

healthy people—or anyone, for that matter—shouldn't be forced to buy insurance they don't want.

But just as with car insurance, health insurance works as a pool in which healthy people subsidize care for the less healthy. If healthier people don't buy insurance, everyone else in the pool must pay higher premiums.

"We need young people to pay into the health insurance system, even though they think they will live forever, and nothing will ever be wrong with their health," Bill Youngblood, an insurance salesman from Rancho Mirage, California, told *USA Today.* "By everyone paying into the system, it helps keep insurance prices stable and more affordable for everyone."

One way of doing this would be to offer a public option through which people without health insurance could buy into a plan administered by the government. Backers of this idea say that the government plan would be more affordable than the ones offered by private companies. While the courts are not settled about whether it is constitutional to require everyone to have health insurance, backers say this is so important that a way must be found.

Emphasize prevention, which would encourage personal responsibility and lower costs by reducing the need for more expensive specialist care and prescription drugs.

The Affordable Care Act already requires insurers to cover many preventive services at no cost. But that doesn't keep many of us from skipping flu shots, delaying screenings for high blood pressure, or avoiding colonoscopies. In doing so, we miss chances to prevent illness or keep small problems from becoming life-threatening—and more costly to treat.

According to this option, we should also accept responsibility for maintaining our own health by eating well and

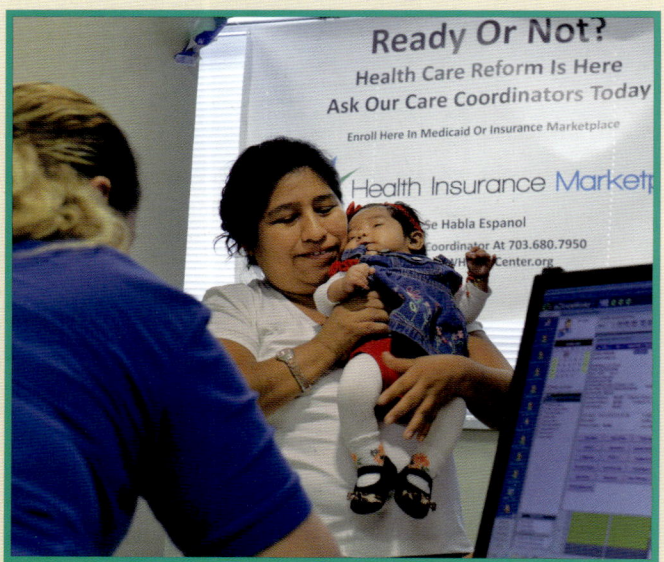

©Jahi Chikwendiu/The Washington Post via Getty Images

exercising. Nearly 40 percent of American adults are obese, according to the most recent federal data. Compare that to Canada (28 percent), Germany (23 percent), France (17 percent), and the Netherlands (12 percent). All have healthier populations and far lower health-care costs. The Milken Institute, an economic research organization, estimated that chronic diseases driven by obesity or being overweight accounted for $480.7 billion in direct US health-care costs.

This option argues that collective and individual actions to improve healthy behaviors have as much potential to lower health-care costs as any efforts at health-care reform.

Require everyone to have a living will—written instructions to guide medical decisions. This could avoid expensive end-of-life care and encourage hospice use instead.

Most Americans say our priority in health care should be to make sure that people who are near death do not suffer. Only one in five Americans think the priority should

be to do everything possible to extend life. Yet a quarter of Medicare spending goes to patients in their last year of life. Some of the most expensive treatments might extend life by only weeks or months. In many cases, patients who do not want aggressive care receive it anyway because they do not have a living will outlining their wishes for end-of-life care.

Medicare made a good start in addressing this situation in 2016. It began reimbursing doctors for advising patients about end-of-life care choices and living wills just as it pays them to give chemotherapy or perform surgery.

This option says we should do more. Everyone should have to provide written instructions to guide medical decisions in the event that they are unable to speak for themselves.

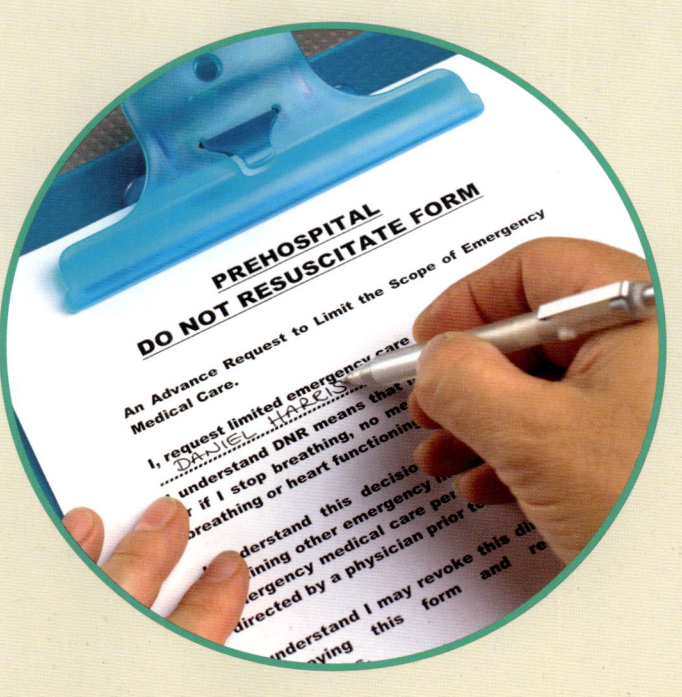

Trade-Offs and Downsides

■ Simply expanding Medicaid does not do enough to fix an unequal system in which the wealthy get excellent care while others get inadequate care or struggle to get any at all.

■ This means people have to buy insurance whether or not they want it or can afford it. Why should people who are young or who take good care of their own health be made to subsidize others?

■ Prevention doesn't control costs. Insurance companies could still charge people and employers whatever they want for coverage, and hospitals could charge whatever they want for care.

■ Requiring people to sign living wills could make them feel like a burden to their loved ones and pressure them to give up care that might extend their lives.

Questions for deliberation . . .

1 Should people have the right to go without health insurance even if this drives up costs for sicker and older people? What should be the consequences for uninsured people who suffer a serious injury or illness?

2 Most people like the idea of more prevention, but will it really help drive costs down if we keep the same complex health-care and insurance system we have now?

3 What do we owe people who choose costly medical care near the end of life even when doctors say that such procedures are unlikely to succeed?

Option 3:
Let People Make Their Own Choices

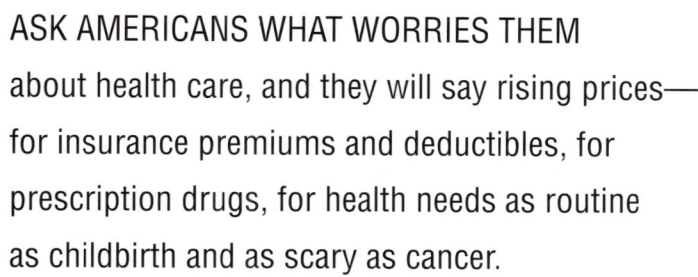

ASK AMERICANS WHAT WORRIES THEM about health care, and they will say rising prices— for insurance premiums and deductibles, for prescription drugs, for health needs as routine as childbirth and as scary as cancer.

"When you have 90 percent of the American people covered and they are drowning in their health-care bills, what they want to hear from politicians are plans that will address their health-care costs, more than plans that will cover the remaining 10 percent," Drew Altman, president of the nonpartisan Kaiser Family Foundation, told the Associated Press.

This option says the most important way to improve our system is to bring down prices. And the best way to do that is to give citizens the responsibility for making their own choices. No one should have to pay for coverage they don't want or don't think they will need.

Some people want just enough insurance to cover a medical catastrophe. This option says that no-frills plans, which cost less and offer fewer benefits, should be made available without restrictions.

The cost of comprehensive insurance can be a burden even to those who have job-based coverage. But it can be out of reach for those buying individual policies. According to a recent Kaiser Family Foundation study, the least expensive comprehensive plan for a 40-year-old single man in Atlanta was $371 a month. The cheapest no-frills plan cost $47 but was available only short-term and to people under age 30.

Americans should be able to choose the health plan that is best and most affordable for them or go without insurance if they don't want it, according to this option. Taking more personal responsibility by choosing high-deductible plans or fewer covered benefits, can even lead to savings by spurring individuals to choose their doctors and providers more carefully.

This option says making prices publicly available and easily understandable would bring down costs by allowing health-care consumers to make their own choices, thus driving competition among providers.

In other countries, patients are told costs in advance. "There are prices on walls in doctors' offices in France. In Australia, people are entitled to binding estimates before they go in for elective surgery," said Dr. Elisabeth Rosenthal, editor-in-chief of *Kaiser Health News.*

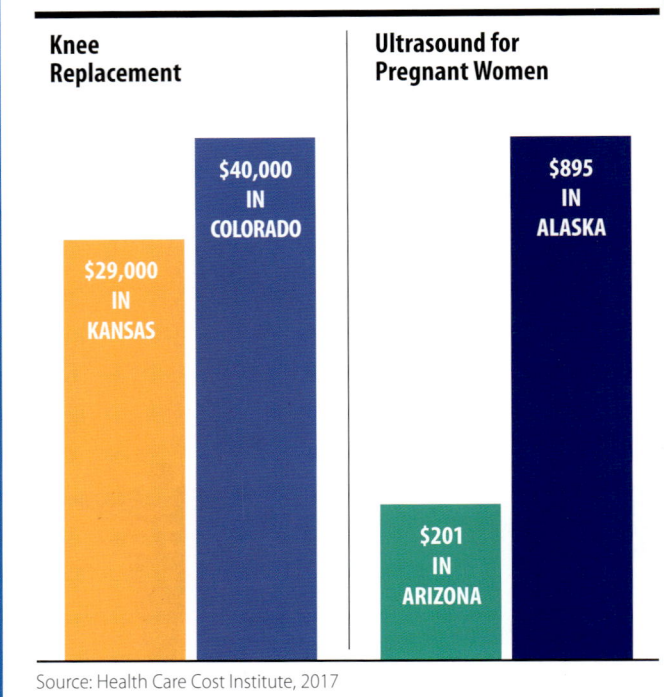

What You Pay for Health Care Depends on Where You Live

Knee Replacement

$29,000 IN KANSAS

$40,000 IN COLORADO

Ultrasound for Pregnant Women

$895 IN ALASKA

$201 IN ARIZONA

Source: Health Care Cost Institute, 2017

People who can't afford care can still fall back on a safety net of public hospitals or emergency rooms. This option argues that the best way to bring about high-quality care at affordable prices is to give Americans the freedom and the information to choose what's best for them.

A Primary Drawback of This Option: *Many people with little or no insurance will develop health problems or die of diseases that could be treated if caught early. Neglect leads to higher costs in emergency rooms and public hospitals, for which we all end up paying. And this option does not directly address overall costs.*

What We Should Do

Make insurance more affordable by allowing people to buy plans that offer fewer benefits.

Under the Affordable Care Act (ACA), insurers are required to cover at least 10 "essential" benefits, including prescription drugs, maternity services, mental health care, and substance abuse treatment, along with certain preventive services. Recent changes, however, also permit less comprehensive plans that cover fewer benefits. These can be purchased for up to a year and are renewable for up to 36 months. This gives people more choices, and backers of this option say this kind of deregulation is needed. It's not fair, they say, to make younger, healthier people subsidize those who need much more expensive health care.

These no-frills plans often cap care at $250,000 to $2 million and may not cover drugs or services such as maternity care. But current rules require those risks to be explained in advance so people can make informed choices. People—not the government—should decide what risks are acceptable to them.

And consider the alternative. In some markets, individual policies that offer all the benefits required by the ACA have gotten too expensive for some people. This means they have to drop their health insurance altogether. A stripped-down plan is better than no plan at all.

Require hospitals, doctors, and drug companies to clearly show their prices.

Imagine buying a new car and, two weeks later, getting a bill for what it will cost you. How can you negotiate a lower price or shop around to find a better deal after you've already driven the car home?

This happens to people who need health care all the time. Seventy-five percent of health-care consumers surveyed by VisiQuate, an analytics firm, said they did not know what their costs would be until *after* they had already received the medical treatment.

"If you don't know the price of the service that you are buying before you buy it and you don't have the ability to compare that to others and determine the value of that purchase, then how is that a functional market?" said Connecticut-based health-care economist François de Brantes in *Modern Healthcare* magazine.

A 2019 rule required hospitals to post list prices of services online, but hospitals complied by posting confusing spreadsheets of abbreviations, medical codes, and numbers. A new rule, slated to go into effect in 2021, tries to get at what patients actually pay. It would make hospitals disclose the discounted prices they privately negotiate with each insurance company as well as the prices they would charge someone paying cash. Hospitals and insurance companies immediately challenged this new rule in court.

This option says that giving people information to make their own decisions will spark competition and drive prices down. The United States should make the health-care system more transparent and protect patients from surprise bills by posting prices.

Allow employers to give workers tax-free money to buy health-care plans on their own in place of a company plan.

The mostly job-based system we have now doesn't really offer people choices. Employers choose an insurance plan, and workers take what they're offered. Most employees don't get much say over whether the doctors they like will be in network, which benefits will be covered, or what any of it will cost.

This option says that employers should offer employees tax-free vouchers to buy their own insurance. That way, people who have health issues or just want peace of mind can shop for a comprehensive policy that covers preexisting conditions. Others, who may be younger and healthier, can choose a more affordable plan and save the rest of the voucher for future medical needs. Employers, freed from the expense of administering health benefits, could pass on those savings through larger vouchers or higher salaries.

According to this option, giving employees tax-free money to buy insurance would both increase choice and reinforce people's responsibility to seek more cost-effective care.

Increase the tax breaks for people who want to put money into health savings accounts.

Americans who are enrolled in a qualified high-deductible health insurance plan are allowed to put aside money in a tax-free savings account to use for medical expenses. People decide how much to contribute to these accounts each year up to a government-set maximum. The money rolls over year to year, so people do not have to worry about losing their savings.

But until people reach their deductible, rules limit these accounts to paying for preventive care and care for some chronic conditions. Most doctor visits and prescription drugs have to come out of regular savings or weekly paychecks.

This option says that restrictions on who can save, how much they can save, and what they can spend their savings on should be relaxed to encourage more people to participate. As we live longer and face decades of future health care, the more saving that can be encouraged, the better.

Lauren Nieves-Taranto and husband Francisco play with their youngest child Nicolas at their home in Windermere, Florida. They were able to cover the entire $8,000 bill from the birth of Nicolas with money they had saved in a health savings account.

©AP Photo/John Raoux

Trade-Offs and Downsides

■ Stripped-down plans may not catch health problems early enough or cover unexpected illnesses and injuries. People could end up with more complicated, expensive conditions that their plans won't cover.

■ People who are sick or injured don't have the time or inclination to comparison shop for treatments. Posting prices could also drive prices higher once some providers realize they are charging less than their competitors.

■ People are often confused by insurance plans. Few of us have the know-how to understand and compare the various benefits and limitations of competing insurance plans.

■ Increasing tax breaks for health savings accounts will give just another tax benefit to the wealthy. Many people struggle just to save for retirement, let alone for unexpected and potentially huge health-care bills.

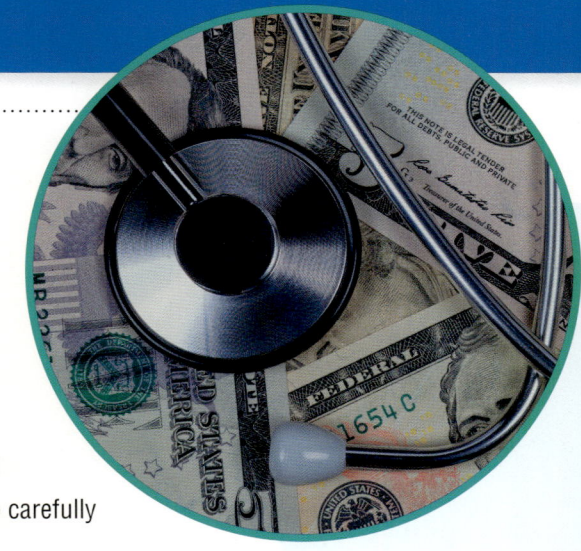

Questions for deliberation . . .

1 How realistic is it to expect people to shop around for insurance plans? Are most insurers clear about what they will cover? What should happen if they aren't?

2 Do people have the knowledge to choose wisely among doctors and hospitals? Is it fair to ask people facing life-threatening situations to carefully weigh costs?

3 This option argues that people who don't need many health-care services shouldn't have to pay for them. But experts say costs will rise for older and sicker people if healthier people aren't in the pool. Is it fair to require healthy people to buy coverage they don't see a need for?

Closing Reflections

AMERICANS ACROSS THE POLITICAL SPECTRUM face a daunting set of challenges in trying to lower health-care costs while still getting the care they, their loved ones, and their communities need. It is important to think carefully about what matters most to us and what kinds of decisions and actions will enable our communities and country to thrive.

Before ending your forum, take some time to revisit some of the choices and tensions the health-care issue presents for us. For example, how does your group weigh these choices?

- If we create a single government program to pay for everyone's health care, would taxes rise and quality suffer?

- Can gradual reforms hold costs down and still get everybody covered?

- Should we take responsibility for our own choices in a more transparent and competitive marketplace even if that means those who make poor decisions will suffer the consequences?

Some important questions to consider are: What do we agree on? What do we need to talk more about? Whom else should we hear from? What more do we need to know? What might we do in our community or in the United States as a whole?

Summary

Option 1:

Ensure Health Care for All

This option says that all Americans deserve health-care coverage and the fairest way to provide it is to create a single public health insurance program similar to Medicare that covers everybody. Our current confusing mix of private and public payers leaves even many people who have insurance struggling to afford co-pays, deductibles, premiums, and out-of-pocket expenses as well as worried that they will lose their coverage altogether. Every developed country except the United States provides its citizens with some type of universal coverage that includes both health services and protection from unaffordable costs. Health care should not depend on a person's income, job, or medical history.

A Primary Drawback

This drastic overhaul would eliminate private, job-based insurance that now covers 181 million Americans and create a huge new government responsibility and bureaucracy.

ACTIONS	DRAWBACKS
Immediately bring the 28 million people who do not have health insurance into a new public plan similar to Medicare. No American should have to go without insurance.	The United States is already deeply in debt and can't afford a new government benefit. Expanding Medicare could divert care from the seniors and people with disabilities it was created to serve.
Move people with private and job-based insurance onto the public plan. Having a single payer will simplify our complicated system and save on paperwork and administrative costs.	Forcing people onto a Medicare-like plan whether they want it or not would upend our entire health-care system. Individuals and employers may save on premiums but may well have to pay new taxes.
Use government's enormous purchasing power to force hospitals, doctors, and drug companies to drop and hold down prices.	Since the government pays less, this could discourage people from going into the medical field and lead to doctor and nurse shortages.
Outlaw astronomical jury awards for malpractice. The fear of lawsuits drives doctors to order unnecessary tests and pass on the high costs of malpractice insurance.	We will lose an important way of making sure doctors and hospitals are more careful. Medical errors kill up to 250,000 Americans a year.
What else?	**The trade-off?**

Summary

Option 2:

Build on What We Have

This option says we should fix what's broken about health care—not destroy the whole system currently in place. Improving the mix of private and public options we already have is the safest and least disruptive way to bring down costs and still get the good health care we deserve. To cover more people and protect patients from high prices, we should strengthen and build on the 2010 Affordable Care Act. Its reforms already require insurers to cover preexisting conditions, make many preventive services free, and cut the percentage of people who do not have health insurance from 14 percent down to 9 percent.

A Primary Drawback

Keeping the private insurance system we have now means continuing to waste billions of health-care dollars on profits, advertising, duplicative paperwork, and red tape.

ACTIONS	DRAWBACKS
Expand Medicaid in every state to cover not just the very poor but also working people without insurance.	This maintains a system in which the wealthy get excellent insurance while others must use Medicaid, which many doctors won't even take.
Require everyone to have health insurance so it will be more affordable overall. When everybody pays in, healthy people help pay for those needing more care.	This requires people to buy insurance whether or not they want it or can afford it. Why should people who are young or who take good care of their own health subsidize others?
Emphasize prevention, which would encourage personal responsibility and lower costs by reducing the need for more expensive specialist care and prescriptions.	This doesn't control costs. Insurance companies could still charge people and employers whatever they want for coverage and hospitals could charge whatever they want for care.
Require everyone to have a living will—written instructions to guide medical decisions. This could avoid expensive end-of-life care and encourage hospice use instead.	Making people sign living wills could make them feel like a burden to their loved ones and pressure them to give up care that might extend their lives.
What else?	**The trade-off?**

Summary

Option 3:

Let People Make Their Own Choices

This option says we should keep government out of health care and give Americans the power and responsibility for making their own decisions. This is the best way to get costs down without giving up our freedom. People should be able to choose the health insurance plan they think is best and most affordable for them or go without insurance if they don't want it. To make good choices about treatment, they need clear information up front about what things cost and better incentives to budget and save in advance. People who can't afford care can fall back on a safety net of public hospitals or emergency rooms.

A Primary Drawback

Many people without insurance will develop health problems or die because they don't get regular care. Neglect leads to higher costs in emergency rooms and public hospitals, which we all end up paying.

ACTIONS	DRAWBACKS
Make insurance more affordable by allowing people to buy stripped-down plans that offer fewer benefits. No one should have to pay for coverage they don't think they will need.	Stripped-down plans may not catch health problems early enough or cover unexpected illnesses and injuries. People could end up with more complicated, expensive conditions that their plans won't cover.
Allow employers to give workers tax-free money to buy health plans on their own in place of a company plan. This will lower business costs while promoting choice and responsibility.	People have little experience or leverage in negotiating complex benefits and prices. Few of us have the know-how to understand and compare competing plans.
Require hospitals, doctors, and drug companies to clearly show their prices. Giving people information to make their own decisions will spark competition and drive prices down.	People who are sick don't have the time or ability to comparison shop. This could also drive prices higher once some providers realize they are charging less than their competitors.
Increase the tax breaks for people to put money into health savings accounts. This will encourage them to plan and save for future health-care costs.	This will give another tax benefit to the wealthy. Many people struggle just to save for retirement, let alone for unexpected and potentially huge health-care bills.
What else?	**The trade-off?**

The National Issues Forums

The National Issues Forums (NIF) is a network of organizations that bring together citizens around the nation to talk about pressing social and political issues of the day. Thousands of community organizations—including schools, libraries, churches, civic groups, and others—have held forums designed to give people a public voice in the affairs of their communities and their nation.

Forum participants engage in deliberation, which is simply weighing options for action against things held commonly valuable. This calls upon them to listen respectfully to others, sort out their views in terms of what they most value, consider courses of action and their disadvantages, and seek to identify areas of common ground for action.

Issue guides like this one are designed to support these conversations. They present varying perspectives on the issue at hand, suggest actions to address identified problems, and note the trade-offs of taking those actions to remind participants that all solutions have costs as well as benefits.

In this way, forum participants move from holding individual opinions to making collective choices as members of a community—the kinds of choices from which public policy may be forged or collective action may be taken, at community as well as national levels.

Forum Questionnaire

If you participated in this forum, please fill out a questionnaire, which is included in this issue guide or can be accessed online at **www.nifi.org/questionnaires**. If you are filling out the enclosed questionnaire, please return the completed form to your moderator or to the National Issues Forums Institute, 100 Commons Road, Dayton, Ohio 45459.

If you moderated this forum, please fill out a Moderator Response sheet, which is online at **www.nifi.org/questionnaires**.